P9-CEU-456

Frontier Home

RAYMOND BIAL

Harcourt

Orlando Boston Dallas Chicago San Diego

Visit *The Learning Site!*

www.harcourtschool.com

This edition is published by special arrangement with
Houghton Mifflin Company.

Grateful acknowledgment is made to Houghton Mifflin Company
for permission to reprint *Frontier Home* by Raymond Bial.
Copyright © 1993 by Raymond Bial.

Printed in Singapore

ISBN 0-15-314441-6

2 3 4 5 6 7 8 9 10   068   03 02 01

This book is dedicated to my children,
Anna, Sarah, and Luke,
and to children everywhere
who love to look into the past

Imagine traveling in a Conestoga wagon through deep woods abounding in shadows and mystery. Early Americans did just that, forsaking the relative safety of the East for an uncertain future on the frontier. They made such slow progress they usually had to leave by late winter in order to find a homesite, build a cabin, and harvest a crop before cold weather set in again.

Jolted by every rock and root, they rode along for days or weeks, tree branches swirling over their heads. Occasional patches of snow persisted in the hollows and along creek beds, and they suffered from the cold. Yet, as the wagons creaked along, they were transporting not only the pioneers' fears but their expectations for a better life as well.

Settlers came from all walks of life, but they shared a common desire to build homes for themselves in this new country. In so doing, they were offered a rare opportunity to achieve freedom, independence, and a better life. Yet with opportunity came phenomenal difficulties, including threats from the weather, disease, wild animals, and sometimes from the Indians who were being displaced. And pioneers could bring very little of civilization's comforts and protections with them—Conestoga wagons were just large enough for a single family, a few necessities, and nothing more. The settlers' lives depended on bringing along the right supplies and equipment and being able to make everything else they needed. Anything that could be made out

Father met us here with two yoke of oxen and an ox wagon. We brought very little besides our bedding and clothing, but it was necessary to pile box on top of box. We left room in front for Mother and for the eight children under seven years of age. The rest walked the hundred miles to the Neosho Valley. We were two weeks making the trip. The oxen were slow; we were heavily loaded; and when it rained we would not break camp.

— *Melissa Genett Moore, Kansas Territory, circa 1860*

on the frontier, even wooden handles for tools, was left behind. Pioneer families quickly learned that they would have to rely on their own courage, hard work, and ingenuity to provide themselves with food, shelter, and clothing.

The land they settled, the American frontier, extended from the Appalachian Mountains to the Pacific Ocean. By the late 1700s and early 1800s, settlers had established farms and

villages in the thick woodlands of Ohio and Kentucky. As this land filled with people, new settlers pushed into what is now Indiana and Illinois, occasionally breaking into a strange, open country. At first this land, which French explorers had called prairie, was little more than an interruption to the trees. However, as they proceeded westward, the settlers encountered prairie more frequently, interspersed with clusters of woods and stretches of river bottom lined with trees.

By the 1830s most of the land up to the Mississippi River had been settled, and the homesteaders moved on to the Great Plains and eventually across the entire continent. The pioneers needed wood for shelter, fuel, and tools. Wherever possible, they settled in or near dense woods or along wooded rivers.

One of the homesteader's most important tools was the ax. Its blade kept very sharp, this versatile tool was used to clear wooded land—as well as to split the huge amounts of firewood needed to keep warm through the long winters. Most often, pioneers cleared fields for crops even before they built a house for themselves. Initially, they slept in their covered wagons, stayed with a neighbor—if there was one—or put up a rough shelter.

Rather than cut down trees, they often "girdled" them by cutting a ring around the bark of the trunk so the sap could not flow up into the branches. The leaves withered and the trees died, allowing sunlight to reach the soil for planting. Or they cut down trees on a few acres, cleaned up the brush, and then had a "log rollin'" at which all the nearby men met for a day, piled up the logs, and burned them. Only after a few acres of corn and a vegetable garden were planted did most settlers begin the construction of their log cabins.

Although log cabins seem as native to America as the land itself, they actually date back to Swedish and German immigrants who settled in the colonies and erected the buildings they had known in their old countries. Modeled after the Swedish design, the earliest cabins on the frontier were made from round

logs about sixteen to eighteen feet long, notched at the ends, and stacked one on top of the other. Later cabins were built more in a German style, with the logs squared into timbers and the corners sawn off even with the walls for a trim look. The gaps between the logs were chinked with wood chips, then daubed with mud, clay, or lime mortar.

If necessary, it was possible for a determined settler to build a cabin by himself with an ax as his only tool. If other settlers lived nearby, they would have a "raisin'" to stack the heavy timbers, often leaving the chinking and other details for the settler and his family to do themselves.

In addition to the ax, other hand tools were used in building cabins. A broadax was used to square the logs and an adz, a tool with a long, slightly curved blade, was used to smooth the logs.

Augers were used to bore holes for pegs to hold rafters and other beams together, since nails were relatively scarce; a hammer or mallet was needed to drive the pegs. Settlers needed saws to cut openings for doors and windows. They used a froe, a tool with a slender blade set at a right angle to the handle, to split logs into boards for shingles and door planks.

The cabin roof was made of overlapping boards or shingles, called shakes, that shed the rain down their slopes. Crude windows were covered with animal skins or greased paper, which kept out the wind and water, yet admitted a faint light.

At first most cabins had only dirt floors. Because the soil was packed hard, these floors could be swept and the cabin kept reasonably clean. Later, settlers added a floor of plank boards or puncheons, logs split lengthwise and laid face up.

The cabin "door" might be an old quilt or hide. Later, when the crops were in, it would be replaced with a plank door, hinged with leather straps or iron. A latch with a string through a hole served as a simple lock. During the day, the string was pulled to lift the latch, but at night it was withdrawn to "lock" the door. It became a symbol of hospitality on the frontier, and to this day people say, "The latch string is always out."

Early chimneys were made of logs stacked one over the other.

Settlers then mixed handfuls of mud or clay from a creek bank with dried grass or pine needles into crude loaves called cats. After sun drying, the cats were laid inside the new chimney and covered with more mud or clay in a "cat and clay" chimney. Although the lining helped shield the logs from flames, the chimneys were still dangerous and caused many fires. As soon as possible, settlers built fireplaces and chimneys of stone or of bricks made from local clay.

The settlers were not able to bring much, if any, furniture with them. Typically, cabins were furnished with tables and benches made of puncheons. They looked rough, but these tables and benches were quite functional and sturdy.

Beds in early cabins were made of poles set into the log walls and attached to crosspoles to form a crude frame. Quilts, blankets, and animal skins were laid over a mattress of dried grass or corn husks. Some homesteaders did not even build beds, but simply rolled up in buffalo robes or blankets and slept on the floor.

If the settlers could afford them, four-poster beds were brought in, proudly placed in a corner, and made more comfortable with straw or corn-husk mattresses. The springs were made of interlaced ropes drawn tight with a wooden tool called a rope key. The saying "Sleep tight, don't let the bedbugs bite" comes from these early beds.

Instead of closets, pegs in the log walls held the family's clothes. Deer antlers were often placed over the door to hold the settler's rifle, powder horn, and pouch of bullets.

The finished cabin was usually a single room, generally sixteen by eighteen feet, sometimes with a loft where the children slept. In this small house an entire family lived, and families were often large, with eight or nine children.

To have six children in less than eight years is something of a record. You would have thought I was in a race to see how fast we could get that new country settled.

— *Grace Fairchild, Dakota Territory, circa 1890*

A fire was kept burning during the day and banked at night, and the air in the vicinity of the cabin was always tinged with the acrid, faintly sweet odor of smoke. The fire was necessary not only for heat and cooking, but as a source of light as well. During the long nights in a strange land, the orange embers provided a glimmer of comfort against the fears that came with the dark.

If the fire went out, it was necessary to borrow a pan of glowing coals from a neighbor. If there were no neighbors, a new fire was started by striking a piece of steel against a flint to make sparks until one caught in some tinder—charred linen or other fine material that catches fire easily. The tinder, along with the flint and steel called a striker, was usually kept in a small metal tinderbox with a built-in candle holder. It took several minutes

or longer to ignite the tinder and transfer the delicate flame to a candle. On stunningly cold January mornings those few minutes must have seemed an eternity.

Once the candle was safely lit, it was held to a handful of shavings or wood splinters in the fireplace. Paper was so scarce and valuable that it was rarely used for kindling. Because it was so hard to start a new fire, settlers carefully banked the embers in their fireplaces with ashes each night so they would always have at least a few hot coals in the morning.

In the evenings the family gathered around the fire for reading, sewing, or playing. In the glow of the fire, the father told stories and the mother mended clothes or made corn-husk dolls while the children played with tops, clay marbles, and other wooden toys.

In some areas settlers lived in constant fear of hostile Indians, and a rifle was needed for defense. Occasionally, homesteaders had to fend off cougars and bears as well. They also depended on the rifle for food: rabbits, squirrels, turkeys, deer, and sometimes even bears provided meat for the table.

Early frontiersmen had always preferred the rifles made by German immigrants because they were more accurate over greater distances than the musket. But the heavy rifles were hard to handle in thick woods, so the craftsmen designed a longer, lighter rifle, also replacing unreliable and at times dangerous flintlocks with firelocks, where a hammer struck a percussion cap. Although the new rifle was made in Pennsylvania, it became known as the Kentucky rifle, probably because it was put to such great use there.

Men made their own bullets from slugs of lead heated to a liquid and poured into molds. The bullets were carried in leather pouches, and gunpowder was kept dry in horns. A smaller horn was used to measure precisely the amount of gunpowder needed in the rifle.

> Flintlocks was mighty good in their day, but they had a habit of bein tricky at times. You had to keep the flint well trimmed and set or it wouldn't knock a spark in the powder pan. Then you had to keep the powder in the pan dry. ... A flintlock had a way of makin a flash of fire, a sizz and a splutter, when the flint struck the steel and knocked a spark in the pan right in front of your eyes.
>
> — *Oliver Johnson, Indiana Territory, circa 1830*

Settlers kept their rifles in a handy place, beyond the reach of the small children, yet close by in the event of an emergency. Boys were taught to shoot at a young age, and women occasionally had to fire the rifle as protection.

On the move west, women brought along the essential cooking ware: iron pots, skillets, and pans; pewter dishes, tankards, and noggins; and some tin cups and utensils. A few pieces of cherished china might also have survived the journey into the wilderness. All other household items had to be made by the settlers themselves. Wooden spoons, bowls, and other items were all carved by hand, often by the boys in the family.

Women cooked all meals in the fireplace. Soup or stew was simmered in an iron pot suspended over the fire on an iron arm called a lugpole. Bread was baked and food kept warm in a kettle with legs placed at the edge of the fire and completely covered with hot coals and ashes. Women also used a "spider," a frying pan with an unusually long handle that helped keep them from getting burned.

Along with hunting wild game, settlers also gathered wild fruits. But they relied most heavily on corn for food, with standard meals consisting of salt pork and corn bread. Pounded or grated to make meal, corn was filling and easy to store through the winter.

Believing in the saying "Waste not, want not," pioneers utilized the entire corn plant. Pigs ate fresh husks, and dried

husks were used in mattresses and woven into mats. Husks were even woven into horse collars, while stubs of corncobs were used as corks in bottles and to scour pans. Meat cooked over a corncob fire had a wonderful flavor, and the ashes from cobs were used as baking powder.

Women raised many other vegetables in their gardens, including beans, squash, onions, turnips, cabbage, and large amounts of Irish potatoes grown in fields. All of these vegetables were nutritious and kept well when pickled or stored in a corner of the cabin away from the fire.

Fruits were sun-dried or turned into jellies and jams sweetened with honey or maple sugar, then poured into crocks and sealed with mutton fat. An animal bladder or greased paper was then tightly stretched across the top of each jar.

Women also grew their own herbs and seasonings, which they collected in the fall and hung to dry. The herbs were then folded in brown paper and stored in wooden boxes.

For their first planting, homesteaders had to bring seeds with them, after which it was critical that they set aside seeds for the following year. The seeds were carefully separated, dried, marked, and then stored in gourds in a high, dry place away from rodents. As more settlers arrived, they could swap seeds with their neighbors to vary the crops.

Since sugar was scarce, settlers often used honey as a sweetener. At first they sought out the hives of wild bees. Soon they learned to keep bees in braided straw hives or in apiaries called skips, usually with loose straw on top to shed the rain.

Domesticated livestock provided milk, eggs, and meat, as well as cheap labor. Homesteaders either brought or bartered with neighbors for oxen, hogs, sheep, geese, chickens, and perhaps a cow.

Chickens were kept primarily for eggs; settlers preferred to eat turkey, deer, and other wild game to supplement a boring diet of smoked and salted pork. And chickens did not need much feed because they devoured just about anything—worms, grasshoppers, even maggots.

Oxen was the main work animal. . . . They was slow, but they could stand the heavy work better'n horses. They wasn't so fretful in a new ground full of stumps and roots. They could be turned out to look for their food and would browse on what a horse would go hungry on.

—*Oliver Johnson, Indiana Territory, circa 1830*

Similarly, the settlers' half-wild pigs—so skinny that they were called razorbacks—ate anything from table scraps to wild nuts. In the evenings, the pioneers needed to put out only a little corn to keep the hogs coming back to the homestead. Hogs were butchered in the autumn, the settlers using every part of the animal. The hams were smoked and the fatty slabs cured into bacon; the intestines became casings for sausage; and all the fat was saved as lard for cooking. The meat was sun-dried, pickled in brine water, or covered in salt and smoked over a low fire.

Salt was necessary to preserve foods, but it was relatively scarce and expensive to buy from traders, so homesteaders often traveled many miles to find natural deposits. Because these places were also used by deer, they were called salt licks.

The men had to make many of their own wooden tools, and their cabins served as workshop as well as home. Pitchforks and rakes were carefully fashioned from strips of wood. Spades were painstakingly carved out of large blocks of wood, and plow blades were sometimes made of very hard woods fitted with metal tips. Even watering troughs were chiseled out of thick logs.

Settlers also used wood to build sturdy fences to protect their crops from animals, including their own hungry hogs and

chickens. Animals were actually fenced *out* and crops fenced in.

In one of the most popular types of fences, long, straight cedar, oak, ash, or chestnut logs were split into quarters or eighths and laid in a zigzag pattern that didn't require nails and was easy to move as settlers expanded. Board fences lined with bushes were also used to keep small animals out of gardens. But nothing could keep white-tailed deer away from the young sprouts, and crops had to be vigilantly watched.

Women made most of the clothing for their families. But first they had to raise sheep for wool and grow flax for linen threads.

In the spring, the sheep were herded into a nearby creek and thoroughly washed; then their wool was sheared off, combed, or carded, to straighten the fibers, then spun into yarn on a large spinning wheel. The yarn was next wound into coils called skeins and dyed, using roots, barks, nuts, and flowers, such as goldenrod or walnut husks.

Linen was made from flax plants. The ripe plants were harvested and the seeds combed out with a tool called a ripple. The stems were then soaked in water, allowed to dry, and pounded with a paddle-like tool called a brake until a silky thread was separated. The delicate fibers were spun on a small spinning wheel to make linen thread.

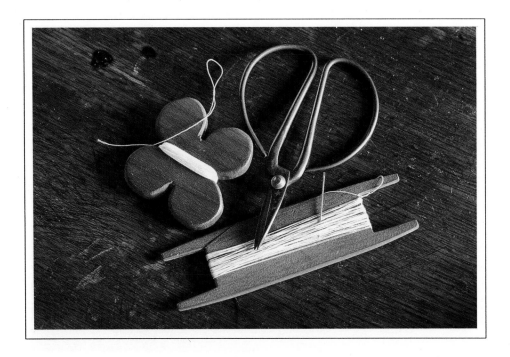

Most women wore petticoats and long dresses of linsey-woolsey, a homespun blend of wool and linen cloth. All married women wore day caps and, when outside, both girls and women wore bonnets to shade their faces from the sun. In cold weather they wore wool or linsey-woolsey shawls.

During their first years on the frontier, some boys and men wore deerskin shirts and pants. The hides were dried, soaked in hemlock and oak bark, then pounded and kneaded until soft. However, men most often wore rough shirts and trousers of wool or linsey-woolsey.

During the winter, some boys and men preferred fur caps, such as the popular coonskin cap, but most often they wore hats made from wool or beaver felt. In the summer, they switched to hats woven from straw or corn husks.

Children and many adults went barefoot in the summer. When cold weather set in, they wore moccasins, or leather shoes made by the father or an itinerate cobbler. There were no left and right shoes—only identical pairs that had to be broken in by the wearer's feet. Making one pair at a time, the father started with the parents and the youngest children, leaving the older children until last.

Sometimes us older boys would go to school half a term bare-footed. On frosty mornins we would heat a clapboard before the fireplace until it was almost charred, stick it under our arm and run through the frost until our feet began to sting. Then we threw the clapboard on the ground, stood on it until our feet warmed, grab it up and make another run.

— *Oliver Johnson, Indiana Territory, circa 1830*

If they weren't making or mending clothes, women were busy scrubbing them with homemade soap. To make soap, water was poured over ashes saved in a wooden barrel until lye dripped from a hole in the bottom. Tallow was made as hog fat was added to the lye, and the goopy mixture was poured into a flat box to harden.

To make laundry soap, ammonia and borax were added, while bayberry was used to make soap for washing up; pioneers seldom bathed, believing that baths removed the skin's natural oils.

Girls and women also made candles for the cabins, pouring wax into molds or repeatedly dipping wicks hung from a stick into a kettle of hot tallow, letting the candles cool between dips. They were then hung up to harden into the brown candles that flickered against the dark of many a long night.

The lives of the settlers were not all work, but even their pastimes revolved around labor. They would get together for quilting and husking bees, and once the work was done, they would have a large meal and a rousing dance.

Children enjoyed many toys—many of them made by the settlers themselves—including corn-husk dolls, wooden tops, and clay marbles. Adults also played games such as checkers with a homemade board and slices of corncob.

Along with the hard work of providing for themselves, the homesteaders faced many dangers, including attacks from Indians, but none so extreme as sickness and disease. Malaria, which the settlers called ague or "the slows," was a part of daily life. They thought it came from damp marsh air, but the disease is actually carried by mosquitoes. Typhoid, smallpox, cholera and other serious diseases swept across the frontier, wiping out Indians as well as settlers. Women cared for the sick, using their own home remedies. Even when doctors arrived on the frontier, they were not always close by.

Very often freedom and opportunity required the ultimate sacrifice, and children suffered most deeply. In the pioneer cemeteries scattered throughout the West, most of the graves are those of children.

With the thought of Indians still haunting my dreams, there was another horror which presented itself too frequently to be pleasant. It was the knowledge of being on the opposite side of the river, without a bridge and away from a doctor in case of sickness.

— *Jennie Osborn, Kansas, circa 1870*

Yet these rugged homesteaders persevered. By the late 1800s most of the West had been settled. Change came swiftly on the frontier, and within a few years, villages with gristmills as well as blacksmiths, coopers, and other craftsmen sprang up around the early homesteads. Stores provided cloth goods, dishes, and other household items from such faraway places as Cincinnati, St. Louis, and New York.

Someday, the settlers might be able to build more comfortable homes for themselves and their families. Yet they would always carry within them the knowledge that they had prevailed through their courage, their wits, and their own hard work. In their hearts, they would always be pioneers, building for themselves a new life in a new land.

We felt our hearts stronger and richer for its lessons, and we all look back on that memorable time as something we would not willingly have missed out of our lives, for we learned that one may be reduced to great straits, may have few or no external comforts, and yet may be very happy.

— *Charlotte Van Cleve, Wisconsin Territory, circa 1810*

Further Reading

Excellent articles about pioneer life are presented in *World Book Encyclopedia, New Book of Knowledge,* and *Collier's Encyclopedia,* all of which were sources for this book. The following books were also consulted in the preparation of *Frontier Home:*

Bartlett, Richard A. *The New Country: A Social History of the American Frontier, 1776–1890.* New York: Oxford University Press, 1974.

Hanmer, Trudy J. *The Advancing Frontier.* New York: Franklin Watts, 1986.

Jordan, Terry G. *Texas Log Buildings: A Folk Architecture.* Austin: University of Texas Press, 1978.

Patton, Jane Cade. *Remembrances of a Pioneer.* Paxton, Ill.: Ford County Historical Society, 1990.

Tunis, Edwin. *Frontier Living.* Cleveland: World Publishing Co., 1961.

Wright, Louis B. *Everyday Life on the American Frontier.* New York: G. P. Putnam's Sons, 1968.

Among the many books about frontier and pioneer life, young readers may especially enjoy the following books, a number of which were also consulted in the writing of *Frontier Home:*

Franck, Irene M., and David M. Brownstone. *The American Way West.* New York: Facts on File, 1991.

Gunby, Lise. *Early Farm Life.* New York: Crabtree Publishing Co., 1983.

Henry, Joanne Landers. *Log Cabin in the Woods: A True Story about a Pioneer Boy.* New York: Four Winds Press, 1988.

Kalman, Bobbie. *Early Family Home.* New York: Crabtree Publishing Co., 1982.

———. *Early Settler Children.* New York: Crabtree Publishing Co., 1982.

———. *Food for the Settler.* New York: Crabtree Publishing Co., 1982.

———. *Historic Communities: The Kitchen.* New York: Crabtree Publishing Co., 1990.

Laycock, George, and Ellen Laycock. *How the Settlers Lived.* New York: David McKay Co., 1980.

Acknowledgments

The photographs for *Frontier Home* were made at the following places: Conner Prairie, the Early American Museum (Mahomet, Illinois), Lincoln Log Cabin State Historic Site, Lincoln's New Salem State Historic Site, and Spring Mill State Park.

I would like to express my thanks to the staff at each of these sites for their generous help with this project and for their continuous efforts in keeping the spirit of the past alive. Without the superlative work they do, day in and day out, none of the photographs in this book would have been possible.

I would also like to thank Audrey Bryant, Amy Bernstein, and the other staff at Houghton Mifflin for their efforts in behalf of *Frontier Home* and in support of my work in general.

As always, my deepest appreciation goes to my wife, Linda, who looked after the children during those many days I was out taking photographs or intently working at the computer screen at home.

Sources

The quotations by Grace Fairchild and Charlotte Van Cleve were taken from *Farm Women on the Prairie Frontier: A Sourcebook for Canada and the United States,* edited by Carol Fairbanks and Sara Brooks Sundberg, published in 1983 by Scarecrow Press, Metuchen, New Jersey. Oliver Johnson's quotes were taken from *A Home in the Woods: Pioneer Life in Indiana: Oliver Johnson's Reminiscences of Early Marion County,* by Howard Johnson, published in 1951 by Indiana University Press, Bloomington, Indiana. Alice Dahlin Lund's, Melissa Genett Moore's, and Jennie Osborn's quotes were taken from *Writings of Farm Women,* edited by Carol Fairbanks and Bergine Haakenson, published in 1990 by Garland Publishing Company, New York.